Active Reception

Noah Ross

Active Reception

Nightboat Books
New York

Printed in the United States

ISBN: 978-1-64362-039-8

Design and typesetting by
Rissa Hochberger

Typeset in
Neue Haas Grotesk
and GT Super

Cataloging-in-publication data is available
from the Library of Congress

Nightboat Books
New York
www.nightboat.org

contents

AD MEMORIAM

CINAEDORUM CARISSIMORUM

cheek

BLOOD

SH!T

CUM

GUTS

SPIT

/ / / /

reciprocal as in the social
as in grace as the active devotion to intimate
intimations at lending as reinvesting
in new forms of protocol this is proto-
calling or shedding blips of a message
in the mess or the hall of a hollow slight
depression in the wrinkle of no bubble
butt to this lanky grovel by the stones
of laid cairns left to dimple foreskin of a
backside to prop as here atlas made maps
to trace deep lines of deep end (d)ance the
mutuality of resource all echo location
has no bearing on the balls of this axial
load take this radial node for flanking
side to side backs slide to blank sties
or nouveau code black skies the electric
infrastructure security council names our
greatest ha zard an e- threat a pulse
or seismic or storm earth en event or seaside
or spatial read galactic a co ordinated plug
read data havens & utopia & uppercase
Sex alerts the NSA to yr email once “to wallow
in poisonous come” once “romantic & dark fuck”
“the kiss of one’s death” as once writ large
on self-pen ned obits bound for the
front lawns of high offices lost unknown
for they who c[]ld’[]ve’b[]n all kinds of
mentors fill gaps as the grace of genera
ti(on/ve) [] let access they who r lodged
as gray data prod prayer prod the end of all
prisons read abolition let open all gates be
they rectal or built as environment let
flood all gates as receptacle

/ / / /

/

a subtle pang   an itch or fissure
long & narrow   breed hollow in
the space b(tween)   knees a rest a
measure /   rest   a measure [...]

/

not touching /

myself / being touched / myself / / not milked / but being / milked / not writing / myself / / to be bred / against the rules / of writing / / in a voice / to be / written / of verbs / deponent / that is passive / in form / alone / active / in sense / alone / / this is not a new / line of thought / in the field of / authorial vision / / Experience, though noon auctoritee / / in the Village Voice / Dodie writes the new / millennium / a mixed marriage / reading Kevin / and other queers / performing a new / erotic

writing / a new /

/

frum the tips
of the tips of
fresh sinew l
end a tendon
lest a hair rest
untangled do
ugh of knots
read the code
of shield may
it op/   /en

/

sexual relationship /

between the writer / as top / the reader / as bottom / / which itself / carries over / the authorial / prick of the pen / the power of / inscription / penetrator / of the page / this voice of / power / seeds narrative / a whole host / of histories / / the argument / the claim / the exercise / becomes / is become / a kind of transfer / of power / as seen fit / from top / to bottom / prick / to being / pricked / is it at once possible / at once potential / at once necessary / to invert / dynamics / historied / mad

e sediment / relations / dynamic / /

/

pen   a frame to a chin
           a frame to the chest
close the door it's an entrance
most suited for haunts or my gore
were yu looking for boatbuilders
carpenters   read : joiners

/

in an erotics / of

reversal / can the reader / top the author / can the author / lay it out / a spread / open for reception / this here / authorial / theory / of bottoming / the reader / the audience / a community / of writing / inside / me / bred / in me / in the text / in the act / of writing / this prick / of many / / to top the reader / take them / on the cruise of / predetermined / fancy / on the path / of constructed / plots / whirl me / on the precipice / of device / the tryst / defined / / on the other side / the pleasure of / th

e reader / filling /

/

the mess of dank baths & hot steamers
this guest clad in leather & singlet
of metal hear the vinyl zip a/s/
under late ex harness clamp
my posture wet & dewy |
clamp my posture
wet & dewy

/

themselves / whole /

on the feast / of these littered / paths / on the narrow / lines / of sight / one by one / filling / minds / hearts / entrails / taking it in / guided / by the light of / a luminary / or chased / here / by the promise / of gossip / / like / like / that moment where Duncan / kissed Mariah / at a Creeley reading / still moist on his cheek / on the page / in the letter / in the Manroot chapbook / way of reaching / the kiss / undying / the World / of every page / like / writing from the space of / being kissed / afire

/ moved to / action /

/

cathexis as investment of
personage but prostheses or app
endix my am endments bite
the bullet or the broadside
in the bath room of the
cock were willed hard
saw him suck/ing off the
new guy on the dancefloor

\ /

\
—

/ —

/ /

| /

|||

||| ||| ||| ||| |||

moved to / every page /

a remnant / of that moment / damp / with an excess / of saliva / of cum / / is it writing / from the bottom / when the scriptor / only mimics / gestures / forever / anterior / so the saying / goes / if the author / is constituted / by language / anterior / does / what is scribed / the authorial / rest / in the act / of pen / etration / inverse / of how it's written / no prick / but being / pricked / in being / receptacle / vehicle / for dissemination / if I am created / by the process / of interpretation / in so

/ being / composed of /

/

dome as in / vase as in
/
prepped 4 / that which
/
is hung in me / prepped 4
/
a filling a / grand plug
/
2 stop / leakage fair
/
snuff 2 / cuff reekage my
/
fish is no / fish at hall
/
nor sheath / to sheath
/

/

a reading / standing

under / standing over / bending / at the turn / of a phrase / moving / from surface / to depths / placed / within / realms perpetual / in broadening / / in the rejection of closure / a novel opening / of the bow / els of the bottom / of the page / of the syllable / of the punctum / of a presence / in my mind / in the language / in the very film / of the thing / itself / an agency of / thingness / being ridden / being written / across the bottom / of the page / across the spine / of this here / object / spl

ayed / ready / awaiting /

/

at the venue \

in the coat room \

at the urinal \

mistype ruinal \

mishear yearn all \

blessings of the pier \

on the sands \

one patrol car \

makes tracks toward \

the shore stay \

/back by the \

mouth of the bay blown /

/back by the /

mouth that u [...] /

/

the eye / the yew /

of the matter / to here make meaning / from this disembodied / state / / the intimacy / between us / forged / across letters / beds / sheets / a promise of / quietude / the silence / of this space / for us two / or more / together / thinking with me / flipping me / from side to side / again / again / for us two / or more / pages / enough / to get across / this space / into / somewhere / just for us two / or more / hearing us / voicing / letters together / an invitation / to read me / here / let us / lay / o / pen

/ /

CHORUS :

rest a

measure

CHORUS :

rest a

measure

/

the visour, or cloke
of, contagious   as /// spreads xacrossx
/   // uncontrollably   upside down inside
out animal/human   anatomic that is *arse/neck*
contortion of S's circus boy/   friend as the web of all
web of all liaisons

false apparel is the
myth of the renaissance   this clamp is a clamp with a
function of fetish as the   country of ///
in the ///   in the ///   confused
as category scrambled time &   /// & /// again at the
table of the /// of the

armed *imaginaire*
will not rest easy while   the nation's enemies not
yet made sexual   '///'
at home or /// or   at home while ///
'///' as position /   being that which is placed   be/
hind which in

violent & vir/lent
read as 'submissive'   or 'passive' a
page in the ///   law
prohi/   biting homointer   sexualcourse
in origin for example

for example a /

bove the bower
of our headstand rest   fair growths of /// packed
in spheres of ///   spider
eggs slick sacs of ///   /// of a window
frame o fallow /// br'd long since ///   long since
flown this

room not nearly   so /// I this ///

/

/

an arch to
the squat

to the spot
of a nape

of a breath

[*re/collect*]

/

squirms to
the ear

bristle

neat blessings
gainst

[*this hard edge*]

/

prick of

the pen
sweet mingling [sic]

uncanny
nourish

[*excr//ment*]

/

trace
seed

mortal
germ

wealth
or
weapon

detritus
and
/or

[*penis* &c]

/

drink inky

dust fill m

y entrails

with the sc

roll sweet

as honey in m

y

[*mouth* &c]

/

/

howls rock metallic stems of fixtures deliver an ode to temperance my angel of androgyny winds of the west encroaching an ambience of incorrect grammars a blessing of tongues tied in brittle departures from rambles a brilliance of clamoring

/

/

//\\\
\\//
//\\\

/

/

a clear hi
2 see thru
watr bent

/

backwards
2 feel out
the rocks &

/

the rabble lft
CLNGNG at the
walls of my rectum

/

in test in e
in play nes

xcavation
ting a ritual

clearing of eggs

/

ther r colum
ns 2 this col
on & its hall

/

ways they
r hallowed
in thir bap

/

tismal font in the
flood of seminal metals

/

in test in al

l forms of beatitude

/

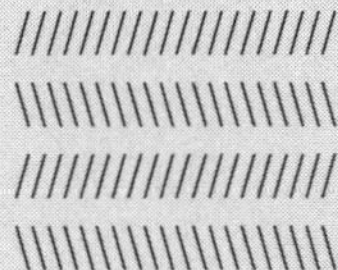

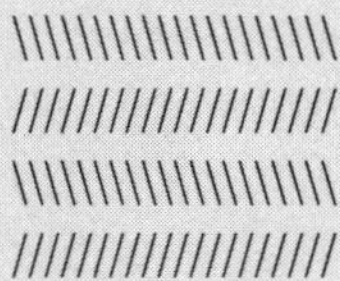

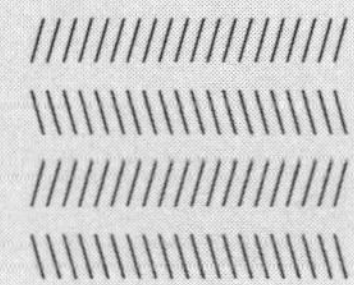

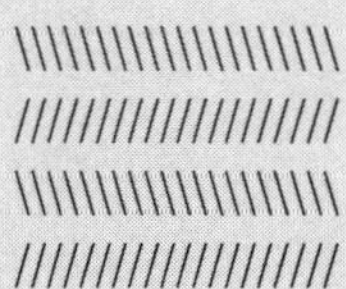

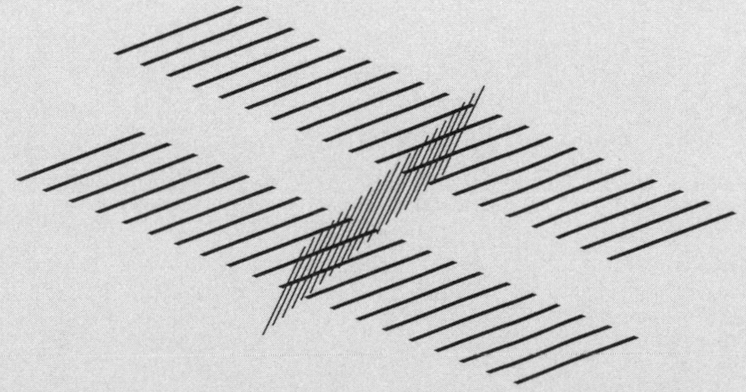

high in our
own bubbles [...]

off the frenetic
sociality off the

table [...]

/

a bark to a
midday libretto

a promenade
of saints & lovers in

the middle of a city [...]

/

taste the distance [...]

metallic trace the [...]

instant erratic the [...]

/

bottom of a jar
rolled under / bed [...] knotted dry [...] (flysch & hair)
had been scattered [...]
& smeared on the
spines of this trade [...] mark managed bi [...]
tradition (bred)

/

jockstrap packed
with the dresses [...] buying a new
phone case or

shoes I'll wear it
out & don't need [...] the box or this
old thing I wore in

/

at the edge of the verbena the echium swallows bees in a lavender bath or olfactory wash for these bitters these fingers edged in yellows drift in thyme crushing sprigs under nails along this promenade these lawns this potted fragrance mellow take it in as an order a numeral a douche for the senses an enema florid this clyster now rare, herbage archaic, sediment of suppository, for fodder rough or coarse or other entryways for fibers in this hall an inflation of sideways facing a maker of daydreams shaker of this here bed or chaise lounge or sofa or basement or cottage, let the soles of these shoes splinter so the heels come in contact with dirt direct as a rod from the ground through tendons, cross the body with roots from the base of the bottom of earthen alignments of dust, take it in, balance of penance, attention to breath, anchor of gaze, extend the senses, the bounds of a body, of its practice, of its potential, disintegration of silvering, of a mirror, or a boundary, between subject // object, language // record, active // passive, life form, be it animal // vegetal // mineral, no tin to this here tin, no metals to distinguish in this bath of the senses, waft of my helpless musk, it has filled columns of the study, sat on pillars in the middle of the city, with the stylites, the ascetics, as a hermit or a dweller in these cosmos for reception, fasting for the intertextual, desire for connection, from a lapse of memory, an abstraction, an association of sediment, squatting atop this city, on its rods, as a spiritual practice, reading grids, or leaves, or grounds, or spreads, of cards, or cheeks, mixed fluids my roots all trade / one another amalgam temptation / in this here lavender linguistics / boots full dirt my present my offering

/

/

the pressure of holding sphincter of holding court of the sphincter hold scepter fair upright sit up right hold scepter fair hold sphincter this is an open court all inquiries will be addressed to those in the choir that is the pulpit of gossip hear now hear with a sigh of several last night's holdings hear the new saga of sages sung clippings these toenails are far too long to make nice plainly far too dulled to anger they are poised & positioned in waiting an act of grace I cruise coffins for steam I cruise coffins for steam

/

hiss orientation the direction of piss hits the dirt by the trellis a relic of burnt roadside clamor // pert midwestern stammer I can hear the yarrow stutter in a mouth or a bowl cut to nowhere o idol of whose matter naught is frivolous the thread spinner hard rot dislodge frum mother bone tends to colon cool it how much would I cover eyes ears mouth every toe and finger not once but many a time

/

of hair flaxen bone decorum of curve vex candid may coptic cures guard the blesséd
of these brambles may propagate
may graft & hybridize
may breed in in//
tolerable climates
may breed in in//
discreet lairs

/

hives creep as ivy the morning glory on the balcony clung tight wrapped the blu columns frum breath it's a snake round a neck · a hand cupped to back pockets · excuse me sir sir sir excuse me sir we don't excuse me sir we don't use our teeth like that in this sir we don't we don't use our claws like that sir in this house we don't bite sir we just – nibble

/

there's a fire reaching peaks of five kilometers somewhere north of here & south of Portland that S could read from the airplane · the older customer called it unfightable might as well go circling yr wheels if there isn't a structure there isn't a chance · S has a friend in New Mexico been doing it so long he's the legend who watches · his mentor's there to speak strategy reporting there's never been a worse season

/

lighting this cliff in my room like a naughty boy sends shots upward in nostrils stuck behind glasses flames tickle · linger kerosene shimmers residual drippage the shorn memory muscles from the agents added · sense triggers a state · like at 16 breaking out frum under/boy pulled the tower when the candle hollered & the family's crystal shattered · it's about time to take the sickness serious now lethargic read · forgetful // not working

/

it's nighttime in Austria where E & his grandmother put the stolperstein in the pavement amidst the hullaballoo of the mayor the local paper they've been planning the ceremony for at least a year now for E's great-great-aunt *deportiert 1942 maly trostinec ermordet 15.6.1942 hier wohnte Julie Spitz* bound in earth thru cement drying to the white rose by the wand of the grotto bind when walking cobbled these stones of the city cobbled behind underfoot above water

/

this third freedom flotilla was raided as expected eyewitness accounts claim the Israeli navy beat passengers stole thousands of dollars & antibiotics from the boat of return there is no return when the phone rings it'll say yr at risk of trespass with these new laws no blood that isn't the blood of power is welcome on the sands of monotheism hear ring maritime law resound across din winds when the warships rode up with the speedboats all masked bound international waters mark & grace innocent passage

/

Dr. Swee Ang writes for Mondoweiss : "we the six women on board *al-Awda* . . . completely humiliate us . . . dehumanize us . . . shocked . . . petty theft and their treatment . . . international women prisoners . . . without decent notice . . . reminded of our vulnerability . . . they would have preferred to kill us . . . of course the publicity . . . that is, if we had been Palestinians . . . while on the seas one week they had shot dead seven wounded more than ninety . . . shut down fuel & food : this is an attack . . . on the ability to defend"

/

al-Awda, Arabic for 'the return' — the name of an organization for the right to return in turn they call for the dissolution of apartheid laws & settlements & demand reparations this week's Torah portion is Re'eh past the closed portion of the sixth reading Moses instructs how to open hands to kinsfolk & neighbors further continuation : if a fellow is sold into servitude, the fellow would serve six years, the seventh go free with parting gifts there is biblical precedent in reparative compensation following periods of servitude that should never have existed in the first place decolonial ropes bind us to local & transnational justice to o//pen

/

the child of bronze age theology & the ghosts of the floorboards & closets I've been gone before seen frum up hi & down lo this rotten garden railed its odor frum windos the veranda testament to trapdoors of the overgrown attic a headspace bless D & bind T in LA, Austin, or back in Poughkeepsie the neo-queer grimoire of gut flora hark the eyes of those who've [] in binding at the wake on Sawtelle amongst kin the constant dribble of the 405 a//drowning

/

I ADJURE YOU by yr powers & yr amulets &
places where you dwell & yr names that just as I take you
so may you take me & bind here this chestful of
jewelry so may I bind us in armor of faeries a queendom
poised at the gates we might open to swallow the
fistfuls of enemies

/

fir//e baptism // thundr perfect

/

with water with the
holy spirit & with fir   e

/

a beloved

to me a cluster

henna blossoms

in the vineyards

/

pigeon grass   vervain
wreathes the   heads for

sympathy a   snapdragon
doghead in   mouths

inhibits   speech

/

a sachet

my spikenard

verdant indeed

is our couch

/

a pebble with   a number
bring me   grapevines

& juniper   myrrh &
frankincense   mastic &

spread linen   the chalice

/

[I am...]

of the natures

[I am...]

(3 lines missing)

/

chrysanthemum in hand knot
grass underfoot together a seal

/

/

pinkwashed Tel Aviv, no, I will not visit / your beaches, your clubs of dispossession

/

/

the grove at the intersection of compass lines, of the business school to the penitentiary to the nuclear lab, at the intersection of state interests, atop a myriad of unknown burials, a likely sacred site, one of many sacred sites of the area, Ohlone sites, disrupted for development, for further displacements, from the shellmound, to this oak grove, a technicality, not within municipal bounds, as the university, identifying as state agency, exists beyond municipality, as in, an exception, as in, an extension, of the federal, on the local, for in this here town, any oaks, with trunks of a certain diameter, protected, in this here town, sitters and stylites, rod squatters perching top thirty-eight coast live oaks, twenty-five pittosporum, eight redwoods, five pines, one or two cypress, cedar, pepper, and yew, how many predated the stadium, all predated the new athletic facility, the longest tree-sit reported, brought forward nearly one hundred arrests or citations, of protestors, sitters, squatters, the university-institution spending upwards of three hundred thousand in police presence, alone, twenty-one months, a record, but by no means exceptional, as in, isolated as incident, the six in Sheffield, the forty-four of the Redwood Summer, Earth First! in Willamette, this is one industry, alone, not to speak of pipelines, of sHell (No) in Portland, hang from bridges, kayak into waters, block boats of transport, shut off valves, rip open whole slithering monsters of steel or plastic tubes buried there are monsters under our own very feet, under our own very cities, towns, plains, farms, highways, waiting, to be torn, open, call it, vandalism, call it, liberation, call it, what you will, what must be done / as an offering / to the offing / of a brazen / eco / no / my

/

/ \

HYMN

/ \

ALL RISE :

/ \

bottom like I

mean it fully all

bullshit no business

just a blessing of act

ive reception in blessing

a fullness of gravity of

cavity laid barren

laid therein stretched

out all the tips and let

hair in deep even deeper

dig til you hit my

ambivalence as an//

i//mal might hear itself

split

/ \

/

I was going to, was going to, do it, that is, by which I mean, stay in bed, like I was supposed to, or at least, for the most part, so-called *should* have, as in, for my health, for the sake of my sinus, my multitude of, sinus, or something, whatever today, is flowing, which wouldn't have even, been my first time, when I write about, bottoming, people ask, if I mean S, and I tell them, with this kind of regularity, like a tick, or an immediate, bodily, reaction, an allergy, my hives, I tell them, *this isn't my first rodeo*, as a joke, rehearsed, amongst many, people, thoughtworlds, friends, strangers, it's all the same, by this I mean, to say, I've been sicker, by much, still, wouldn't stay, in one place, I was thinking, the other day, this afternoon, about racing, in my head, in my actions, there's something, astrological, I'm not, exactly, detail-oriented, at the same time, minute, in focus, it's a paradox, of my essence, one of many, I had this lover, whose signs were, entirely opposed, to one another, a lifetime, of tension, he wears it, well, as a matter, of fact, this one time, the mother of a best friend, had warned her, to take me to the hospital, it was a mixture, of factors, there was the pneumonia, but that only came after, like the hives, after the dose, of the antibiotics, that might've, gotten me there, the first time, but that only came, after, the unexplainable, weight loss, knives to my gut, the sharp abdominals, a sudden gluten, insensitivity, or is it, intolerance, but that only came after, there was the breakup, there was a history, there was something, I read this thing, recently, on functional disorders, a term that's emerged, to discuss, or rather rectify, the language, around the 'psychosomatic,' as in, by which they mean, it's a problem, of history, to claim, *it's all*

/

in yr head, but there's something, going on, with these heads, particularly, in relation, to trauma, tests can detect, absolutely nothing, yet people, clearly suffering, can show symptoms, of a multitude, of possible, diagnoses, shuffling, between doctors, possible treatments, tests, among tests, I wonder about tests, a life built on tests, what's there to trust, anyway, this one time, after being treated for gonorrhea, 'successfully,' I started showing symptoms, again, anew, there were the mornings, full of discharge, at my tip, I could see remnants, sticking dust, or hair, a bit of fluid, this time neither yellow, nor greenish, but still, a pain or burning, sensation, the swelling, an itch, at the clinic on Essex St., caught myself claiming, I was *clean*, after having just written, this paper, on the problematics, of the language, around STIs & 'dirtiness,' I felt so, a certain way, unsure, the shot had been painful, the nurse had said something homophobic, but I wished I remembered the exact wording, something grotesque, regardless, this young queer doctor, at this clinic, appalled at my language, said the tests showed nothing, & it made me wonder, whether the whole ordeal, had been constructed, by the verdict, of results, the symptoms stopped, it wasn't, in my system, the first time, when they said it, was in me, I tried to call, the only guy, who could've passed it, my way, I'd even used a condom, didn't even, really, want it, later, wondered, how it'd, happened, an old friend, passing through, he wouldn't hear me, wouldn't take my calls, respond to texts, he was midway crossing, the country, there were multiple, levels of deceit, I later learned of, but I knew the person, with him, who I told to later find, they'd been together, they got tested, neither h

/

/

ad it, either, they said I'd, had a false, positive, I wondered, but the sun was out, it had been easy, to stay in my head, with this fog, easy, to stay in, my bed, for the sake of, a sinus, or stomach, gut, or cock, or head, or sickness, there's something, to be said, about the flow, of energy, of the emotional, like the gut transfers, its bacteria, across stomachs, across housemates, lovers, friendships, I pick up, my bacteria, willfully, from the people, I love most, it slowly, kills me, I wouldn't really, mind, a death of honor, besides, I've been quite, adaptive, taking in, a multitude, a brethren, having consumed, the flora, a veritable, city, of the minute, the miniscule, sort, of inhabitants, the game, one of playing, host, each surface, each object, body, cell, touched, or in my path, is welcome, is absorbed, with or without, the will to join me, it's a journey, of growth, of continual re-adjustments, in the formula, of my enzymes, of my basins, on this street I touch each plant of the parkways, the rosemary, pungent, the anise of my bluffs, rolled between the thumb & a finger, good to chew on, keeps me busy, all this racing, between work & more work, I synchronize my fingers, the thumb joining each tip in shared order, index finger to the middle, to the fourth, to the final, a dance, is this tick, is this compulsion, watching these hustler films for lines of desire, as a genre, *Speedway Junky* does it perfectly, almost, self-reflexively, the main boy, the speedway junky, wanna-be racecar driver, the straight one, or the one whose sexuality, was never much, in question, certainly masc, the one desired, especially, by the best friend, the queer, Mike & Scott, a love not entirely, reciprocated, perhaps even, understood, in this one, as in *Midnight Cowboy*, the figure of the queer, here the sick, dies, the speedway junkie goes on to his

/

dreams of North Carolina, its fast cars, he wasn't very good at the streets, just passing through, anyway, I like ones where the main character dies instead, even if it's silly, like this one called *Johns*, has this whole life of Christ shtick, I'm not opposed to, it's in the very language, the film of it, a fabric, a coating, it clings to the back of my throat, hangs from the ceiling, lines the parquetry, of pure protein, so distracting, I can hardly get to, my emails, I'm a sucker, for this kind of shit, lines the walls, of my thoughtworlds, something as banal but pricy as a love for green liquors, something as flamboyant as the imprint of a crown of thorns, thorns the crown, these hustler films & debilitation, narcolepsy, or pneumonia, or the mysterious progression, of symptoms, in *My Own Private Idaho*, it's said that various doctors, understand narcolepsy, to have something to do with chemicals, of the brain, while at least in the film, it seems to hit come moments of stress, as the world turns to, historical, personal, traumas, the houses hazy, outlines of some, Idaho, some, place in the potato state, the figure, the hair, of the woman, I've been shitting these crowns that thorn my bottom, thin spirals, they line the basin of the bowl, from my bowel, striking in spots sensitive, from recent exposure, play, the slight sting, is there pleasure without, pain, or the lasting effects, of what was pleasure in the moment, is it pleasure, still, yes, extended, outside of one moment, another, moment, I was going to, was going to, do it, that is, by which I mean, clean the insides, with the help, of a shower, I was sure, I needed it, was sure, there was something, to it, something viscous, something left, over from days, or weeks, or dreams, or mome

/

/

nts in another, time, or space entirely, taken, from conversation, to a memory, there was something, left over, something, viscous, lining the throat, the ass, the memory of, a Tuesday, or weekend, saunter, to the fields of, some summer, yellow flowers, lining pricks, skins, bottoms, of feet, a messenger, harbinger of, another, past, or, presence, with me on, my bus, my commute, in my bedroom, when the door creaks, open, just a, comma, of a pause, so I feel, welcome, I feel so, welcome, in the bath, of my confrontation, awash, in a glow, of recognition, turn the water on, there's nothing, never been, anything, just the haunt, of a presence, in my ass, or in my bedroom, or at the bookstore, when the light flickers, above my head, above the counter, with the faint, odor wafting, not the next door, waffles, but the smoke, that once flowed freely, behind the register, at the banister, among the towers, turn the water on, there's nothing, but the presence, of air, trapped in a bowel, like my rashes, once I started taking notice, with a journal, they were a constant, daily, and nightly, before falling into slumbers, they would coat me, dress me, in the robes of my red castle, we were palatial, til I started, taking notice, with a journal, scribing regal, it was one week of writing, they couldn't take, the exposure, fled my body, with no warning, as quick as they had come, turn the water on, there's nothing, but the outlines of a faint battlefield, along my torso, across my arms, legs, kneecaps, feet, the ghost of past reactions, still inside me, for the most part, still beside me, as I take in, more of the same, as a shimmer, as the possibilities of a hole, I was determined, not to reinscribe, the kind of lack, I found, problematic, that so surrounds, the writing

/

of a hole, its presupposed, relation to an interior, an opposition, to action, agency, a dwelling on want, for its sense of lack, as though what's 'missing,' fuels desire, without question, of an influence, from the outside, be it the social, or the sediment, today I woke up to the jackhammers, nailing the grounds across the street, from my seaside bedside, I live in a beautiful neighborhood, against my expectations, so beautiful developers have been rearing, ugly heads into corner shops, one story homes, determined our lack of levels, of expensive condos, demands construction, it's a kind of logic, I can't wrap my head, round, when I see texture, I don't think of adding, layers to gloss over, foundations, it's as simple as ambience, or hear it, sonorous, as a soundscape, in the minimalist genre, look for timbre, there are colors to each, tone, step, fissure, there is a practice, to uphold, in exposition, so brash to think, one could merely top it, top it, and top it, again, and again, building, it's a horizontal structure, the beauty of its potential, widening, of sound, has something to do with surface, as in area, how wide might we spread tones, cheeks, delays, filters, the wanderer, in the bea(s)t, across speakers, across inputs, across holes, into many ears, into many points of reaching ears, a texture spread across blankets, grounds, dirts, foundations, holy and unholy, at once, many a time, many a timbre, an air, a rest , , many a silence, speaks to more than silence, beyond alienation, there is the (w)hole, matter, of being, together, at once, not ever alone, but together, there has never been, such separation, a language-oriented desire, an object-oriented, subject, a truth that lies in its deceptions, beyond the study, I am pricked, by that which cannot be named, a , , full of gas, how I feel at my day job, my night job, my in between job, where does the

/

/

writing fit in, the sex, we fuck to the open window, to the drones flying above us, around us, not because we want to but because we don't have curtains, we are open, to the plains, to the lawns of the northwest, the lone crow, along fences, sheds, not by choice, we are open, hello neighbors, hello surveillants, we are open, to your viewing, pleasures, in your face, we are defined, by the play, of light, through planes of glass, be it bay, or bow, oriel, supported by corbels, brackets, or a multitude of bodies, muscles, ligaments, pulling me, slowly, quickly, gently, full of force, in one sling, in one fell swoop, supported, by arms, legs, torsos, by the ridge, of a back, of shoulders, extending, to grip, to handle, extending bones, to rip, a ramble, into zones, unknown to fair cartographers, those invested, in the surface, of the matter, exterior planes, what is made visible, to an eye, or for peeping, what here is made for creeping, in my holes, into my hollows, the dugout of a grotto, project me inward, can submit to pressure, path of innards, willful in a filling, alert to the directional, the positioning, an act of the conductor, moving hands, for the orchestra to follow, moving limbs, for the organs, the intestines, to swallow, at the right pitch, in the right, tempo, a choreography, of motion, commotion, disrobe a notion, the full symphony, at my back, behind me, above me, below me, a nocturne for a lazy morning, a prelude for a tryst, a swell of the horns, of the brasses, mark the overture, cue the strings, the vocals, hear a body sing, in the time of two, out of sync, in a temper, an aria of want, full of air, for the other, for the chorus, to respond, watching us, feeling us, the ballet of balls, swinging at my bottom, conducting masses, requiems to my grave

/

(l), this mix of power / powerlessness, receptive / conductive, passive / active, fuels the trumpets, with the cellos, a mid-range low marks the bass for this melody, of maneuvers, mathematical, in precision, hands call, time, call, time for, breath, take a pause, or a moment, of , , plucking me, loose, as a jack, or this string, out of tune, dropping tones, dropping whole steps, beg me lower, take me down, octaves, or a fugue state, here we are, imitative, of our original subject, here recurring, in a mediated fashion, at a different pitch, in a different pairing, the same song, the same tune, the same structure, across two or more voices, contrapuntal, these voices, harmonically interdependent, in contour, in rhythm, independent, this is point against point, prick against prick, fixed, on this place, on this surface, my head against these sheets, these pillows, against points, against pricks, note against note, as suspensions, as florid, if the final is approached from below, the leading tone must be raised, in a minor key, at the cadence, ascending, rules to these steps, countering the firm, contrary in motion, built from the bass, up, built from the bottom, so to speak, this fantasia breaks from tradition, or what is found in textbooks, or canons, breathing heavily, to this grand march, in time, out of sync, in a fugue state, in a haze of brasses, with the resonance, of a string tide, plucked at the soundboard, breathing chromatic, on this scale, put a pedal, to my rails, a flame to the test, to my nest, sharp protrusions, eased in with the cadence, the progression of motifs, instruments, (w) hole sections, fill me, ease me, lubricate the ears with this swallow song we've been working toward, a symphony for this moment, for this miracle of masses, Mayröcker,

/

/

inhabiting Chopin, in letters, says it best, "*I have looked in the eye of the hurricane* and, shepherd of a time signature" from her place made holy, another M, outside, tells us this theory, of the earth's immunoreaction, to humans, as evidenced, by the rate at which, we experience, disasters, of the so-called natural, a bodily reaction, to a fever, to chills, sick in bed, an awareness, imitating the body, or the body imitating, the (w)hole earth, entire, the (w)hole landscape, of sickness, taking on, other traits, of other, landscapes, insertions, of bounds, between memories, of the personal, or the spatial, temporal, here is not I, in a time I've never lived in, on an earth devoid, of sickness, the same, but not, the same, the language, landscape, insertions, inverted, here I am, in a time I've never not, lived through, holy matter, made a rectum, right, having been ruled, governed, steered, guided, honest, here they say proper, a muscle, direct, still breathing, beating, heavily, kneading, lines, from other fugues, into this hopper, death of ego, direct, a marriage of mentality, the storm is the finale, the great march, the climax, to the throes, of a corpus, or many, the body as a work, or a collection, of works, in progress, in motion, in ecstasy, a frenzy, of peaks, an abundance, of fulfillments, lowly, like the number, closest, on the physical plane, to emanations, kabbalistic, I live in a beautiful neighborhood, despite the designs of capital, I can go on a walk, or hop to the tracks, to write a few lines, off my belly, it's a windy day for the water, but these walkers don't stop for less than, rails approaching, a grid that keeps locking, there's no sense to the matter but that wasn't, the question in place, the argument that precedes, a section, the tune that keeps hauntin

/

g, something like nothing, to it, no words no, mind to skew it, just let the body go and, see what it voices, as in not to write it but as in, receive it, as in dictated, active, in reception, I put us down, to the page, here, I hear, my ghosthaunts, my loves lost, my comrades, speak through me, Jack, Kevin, I wonder if you're, together, today this, week, this group, from Glasgow I heard on buses, in middle school this, week, a hymnal this, week, the dogs from each house in the periphery, of numbers, lets loose a, howl, in response to the other, a signal for time, as much, as a marking, of space, the dissonance, in direction, a polyphony, in reception, through the window, from which haven, is this bellow, this, slow dance, a, further, pause, in breath, and motion, a care for, edging, the poem, out, from its, form, that is, a set, of lines, don't break, edging, this motion, in ecstasy, this fugue, its imitations, for peaks, upon peaks, no, control, to the matter, it's been, controlled, from the, start, even, still, bits I can't, keep, hold on, bits, at this, hour, by this, point, long past, mere exposition, the overture, lost, in the frenzy, in the drama, of the who(le), in the temper, of this, slip, in the breath, of the thing, a bloodstream, rush, ing, getting, to the, , where I, won't, ere I, err, I, can't, tr, y, to st, op, the fren, zy, of pe, aks, in ecs, tas, y, beat, ing, heav, ily, knea, ding, th, e, matter, out, of m, y, ha, nds, entir, ely, a diff, eren, t, rh, yth, m, to th, es, e, letter, s, le, t, th, em, r, ip, lik, e, th, e, sen, se, to i, t, fall, ing, to pi, eces, o, n, th, is, gro, und, be, tween, m, y, bu, tt, ock, s, ne, ar, t, o, th, e, pros, t(r)a, te, sen, sing, a, hig, her, vi, bra, tion, dee, per, sen, sa, tion, a wa, y, ou, t, of, , sen, se, to sy, lla, ble, to so, und, to, , o, , to, , o, h, a, h, o, y, es, y, es, to, , o, h, y,

/

////////////////////
\\\\\\\\\\\\\\\\\\\\ e s
////////////////////
\\\\\\\\\\\\\\\\\\\\

o \\\\\\\\\\\\\\\\\\\\
////////////////////
h \\\\\\\\\\\\\\\\\\\\
////////////////////

m

y ////////////////////
\\\\\\\\\\\\\\\\\\\\
////////////////////
\\\\\\\\\\\\\\\\\\\\

\\\\\\\\\\\\\\\\\\\\
e ////////////////////
\\\\\\\\\\\\\\\\\\\\
////////////////////
s

o
h
m
y
e
s

(w)hole

GUTS

BLOOD

SH!T

SPIT

CUM

it is dark now in the hollow at the base of the blanket it is quiet there are only shapes

/

where there are shapes each other swal/loo swa/(olo)wen from swelgan or spelgan as

/

in swallow & incorporate & absorb & imbibe & devour & there r countless co•formations

/

blotting by my witness in flagrante as in blazing w/ in/delicate delineations a noun

/

from the participle of a verbal form of a noun sacred fluids passed from form to form

/

to form found themselves the selfsame in the selfsame base of the selfsame blanket

/

there are the selfsame shapes & countless co•formations blotting by my witness in

/

that most confused cate/glory of yr annals prick the hole of my most loose canon

/

in the dress of the clergy brazen I am against yr basic nature it is somewhere in the

/

bowels of my night-haunts sloping by the virgule hold the little twig let it breathe in

/

the confines of a body basin it has passed the gates of my gates read a hell mouth to

/

nether regions dried as a sand or the husk of our millstones little twig among the

/

countless co•formations rotting by nigh keepers are mere reapers wont to harvest in

/

the ritual of production as a labor there is no right to a rectum has no straightness

/

nothing proper in an etymological steering there are word shapes not the selfsame

/

but the selfsame blank stares cut no stalks this grim heaping let the greens reach high

/

heav'n so the bottom stays our bottom save the throngs of conflagration here wasters

/

want a respite from the bosses of babies in making in the countless co•formations I

/

am stooping to a level headed back room cum shot to nowhere but caverns of the

/

annals of molars there are in-roads & out-roads & by-roads & dry-roads I am hoodl

/

ess in witness bared head to shrift my litmus I am that utterly confused cate/glory

/

notorious & indecent let all crops grow till waste/rot my waist/rot verbatim temptation

/

hark communes of s(p)/oils we are bred bare in the bare bred teeming there are

/

countless co•formations on the banks of rank gesticulations of the sauna or the

/

bathhouse drips are dank as restorations there are the selfsame faces in the selfsame

/

waters are the selfsame traces there is my dust to your dust to our dust where

/

we are place/ /less

/

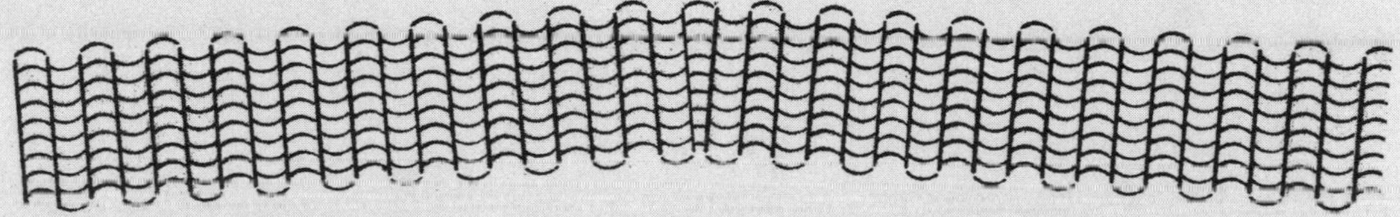

I TAKE IT IN with my morning coffee, in our bed, on the porch, at the kitchen table, with a history, of letters, Dennis, with or without Mark, Kevin, Bruce, Bob, with or without Jack, Hervé, with or without, the presence of, myself, "already an assemblage, a mixture, of liquids, over there," commentary, from nearby, [IRON CHEF], in doing this, looking/feeling backward, I TAKE IT IN, there are tactics, tried & true, a history, of lust, the body politic...

I TAKE IT IN as in open the door, the gate, the windows, on the flip side crossed by the pines of onetime cruisedives, the spines of Wieners, antirelational, & the anti-antirelational, Muñoz on Myles & Schuyler, not merely for investment, in a kind, of utopia, albeit, complicated, at that, as in, ambivalences, everywhere, there is a turn from the negative, altogether, somewhere, some hole, or haven, from death drives...

I TAKE IT IN as I give it, as in, a kind, of versatility, as if, so below, as above, the bower, or my torso, as an archive, as a subject, looking/feeling backward, I assemble, a mixture, of liquids, or dusts, altogether, vibrant, as matter, of fact or refuse, animated, an altar of affect, glued kitsch, a Lanigan-Schmidt, an architecture of diction, comes to life, once inside me, reverberations, abound, in me, abound, from me...

I TAKE IT IN as a poetics, receptive, one Balzac general, and the sister, at the opera, a sort of text, the organ, to them, the most daring instrument of human, grandeur, a whole orchestra, itself, the poem is future, present, and past, it is the possibility of space, routes that fill, born of looking, of feeling, a bottoming of time, open, to vibrations, a tender, touch, a penetration by the page, at the level of, the letter, a sodomy of syllables...

I TAKE IT IN as gusts, that is, a process, I need to disconnect to reconnect, to reconnect to disconnect, slow, that is, steady, a grip, lucky if I can get, an utterance a mumble a murmur a tip, I am open, at each orifice, in waiting, splayed, surrounded, polyphonic, it functions, unto these voices, bent, at many, angles, at many, shapes, numerous, in my approaches, that is, positions, that is, expansive, unto these voices, it functions, I am bent...

/ the *cinaedus* is a problem of gender is a class traitor is a wolf in a king's robe or sheep in an expensive suit or a jock strap under the dressings of power text-meta-text from which time are we spoken to today tonight yesterday a dancer the word itself of the Greek before then still further /

\\

THE APPARATUS is @ work on a new series of portraits in a living room in Texas fueled by the labor of thousands of underpaid workers in factories spanning the rust belt, the bible belt, the borscht belt, below the waist of the frost belt, corn belt, rice belt, unzips the trousers on johnny appleseed, metal sheds across the wastelands of stolen fields, plains, tundras, rolling hills, tumbleweeds, the veranda, immeasurable...

//

THE APPARATUS will incorporate those deemed market-safe into realms of the appropriate in regards to borders made by virtue of the language of inclusivity in the aims of attaining future landscapes, that is bodies, that is capital, into a model predictive of growth, that is, the reproduction of the foot soldier is the reproduction of empire is the reproduction of capital, that is, the reproduction of empire...

\\

THE APPARATUS sets up fronts housed by major corporations to brand the new wave of respectable queerness within certain confines of proper expression the nonprofit cares most about white cis gays in management positions vis-à-vis 'equality' as an index than housing, healthcare, the safety of QTPOC, trans, non-binary, gnc friends, the environment, when Chevron, Goldman Sachs, Monsanto, awarded 100% ratings...

//

/ foreign perhaps Asia Minor implicit that such a word & with it such a position of trouble in gender of trouble classwise could never have been of power no it enabled other powers or later of a nation the blame placed elsewhere on a gendered failure made a dancer made 'exotic' explicit /

\\

THE APPARATUS focuses on the family, on the uniforms, at once desires representation & abhors exposure, directs traffic into, lines into, the STATE, into, cops @ prides funded by salesforce, amazon, google, apple, airbnb, pg&e, uber, whole foods, bud light, smirnoff, rainbow french fry boxes, the game is, one of consumption, material & branded, the corporation is a legal body, says, "I'm an 'ally'"...

//

THE APPARATUS uses western conceptions of gender & sexuality to legitimize conquest overseas, across continents, in regions formerly colonized by the same powers, it is endless, as a loop, of interference, there is FEAR, here stoked, as flames, do breathe, toward violence, here stoked, do breed, a multitude, of violences, a current, discourse, co-opted, there must be, another current...

\\

THE APPARATUS pays off multi-national corporations to extend regimes across continents & in the city getting whiter, how far from the Tenderloin cafeteria?, where the promise of going public has young millionaires squirming to buy boats & long-time community activists itching at the bar over this next round of displacements, won't let them get away with this shit this time, won't give up, the same kinds, of concessions, for this shit, this time, won't...

//

/ ly non-Roman the degenerate general (Plutarch) whatever non-man seeks forever an 'and whatever' (Ovid) a filthier right hand a greedier asshole hairy & sold for a dime (Catullus) split all the way to the navel (Martial) to be dug or plowed (Juvenal) a web of association meaning is /

\\\

From Plato's *Laws* the phrase is rendered *against nature* & even Boswell finds it problematic, or at least perplexing & perhaps has something to do with a distinction b/t the 'man-made' & the 'natural' as in 'what is born' // the 'constructed' or the language of production, in earlier work the natural is all kinds of attraction, the ubiquity of sexual pleasure, there is nothing unnatural about it -- *rightward drift?* -- could tell the story of a phrase, as a genealogy, of employments...

//

Peter Damian writes a book of Gomorrah urging the clergy to stop masturbating, together & alone, performing fellatio, having sex between thighs, between asses, unless this stops with an *IRON FIST*, ruin to many...because a sin against nature is 'a sin against God,' Aquinas considers it more damning than sins against other people, if the enemy is the individual & not the institution, the sodomite & not the rapist, the queer & not the dictator...

\\\

Edward II, either viciously murdered, symbolically penetrated, by *RED-HOT IRON*, otherwise killed, or disappeared, regardless, dethroned, as the public at large, as well as the powers of nobility, strong distaste for his male favorites, the sovereign-being-topped, and by Piers, lowly in class, in garb foreign, and by Hugh, notorious amongst barons, Froissart makes special note of Hugh's penis, severed and burned at his execution, for both sodomy & heresy, severed and...

//

/ transferred from the 'effeminate' & 'Eastern' dancer to the willing bottom to the eunuch priest of the Mother Goddess (*gallus*) Anatolian, Phrygian, all given origin as elsewheres, made the 'effeminate' as 'Eastern' displaced onto a history of the body deemed subservient from the West /

I read somewhere, of two poet-masochists, emailing about Balzac's *La Duchesse de Langeais*, it's something, full of conflicting feelings and gestures, emotional and cruel, strange, if read in a certain way, rad?, one poet-masochist, seductive, tells the story, of the general, time and time again rejected, for a love volcanic, full of fire, it erupts, his thumb to her forehead, she leans in, defiant, her body, hotter than his *BRANDING IRON*, can melt his objects, meld his claims to, power...

The church subsumed when the state took control over punitive measures, a host of virtues, procured, among, the moral subject, the righteous citizen, the divine inspired, law made canon, mandate of political worth, or lack thereof, on account of, there are many, acts, performances, presentations, mark the body, outside the canon, outside the law, mark the body, there are many, acts, to resist notions, of virtue, mark the body, outside the law, outside the canon...

Hocquenghem, in *Homosexual Desire*, displaces the regression said to lead to perversion, onto French penal code, its insistence on acts 'against nature' symptomatic, of paranoiac regression, the reversion, to terms, of condemnation, St. Paul, men forsaking, the 'natural use of women' is fucked up anyway, as language, in the police state, of the nineteenth century, the *unnatural* signals the queer signals the guarantor of desire & of its repression...

/ perspective of empire deemed penetrable from the perspective of empire the state sees the land as open for conquest the state sees (   ) / as enemy, many others with which to organize, coalition of not-my-enemies, many others already leading, a problem of power, a problem of genre, a crisis, then sex was a party trick, in revels under control, the genre contained, but what of when it isn't +
more (   ) /

CHORUS :

rest a

measure

WHAT is the middle of the thing, WHAT
are we, of ages?

CHORUS :

rest a

measure

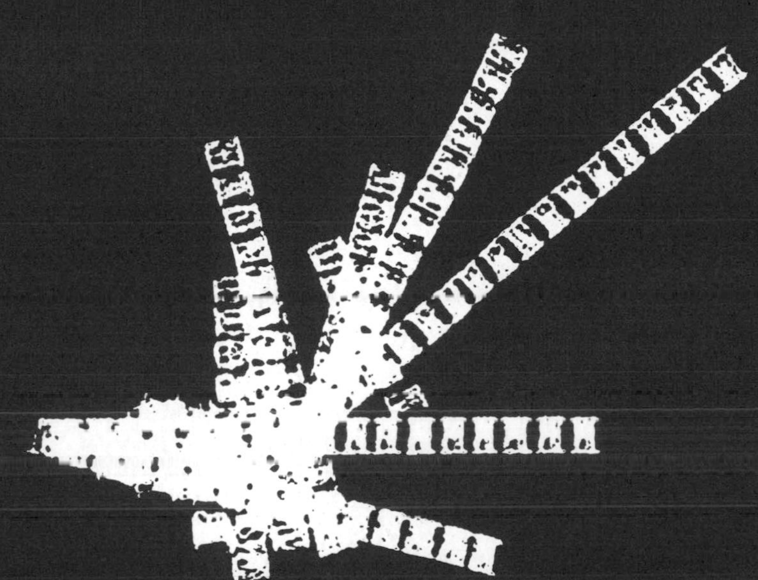

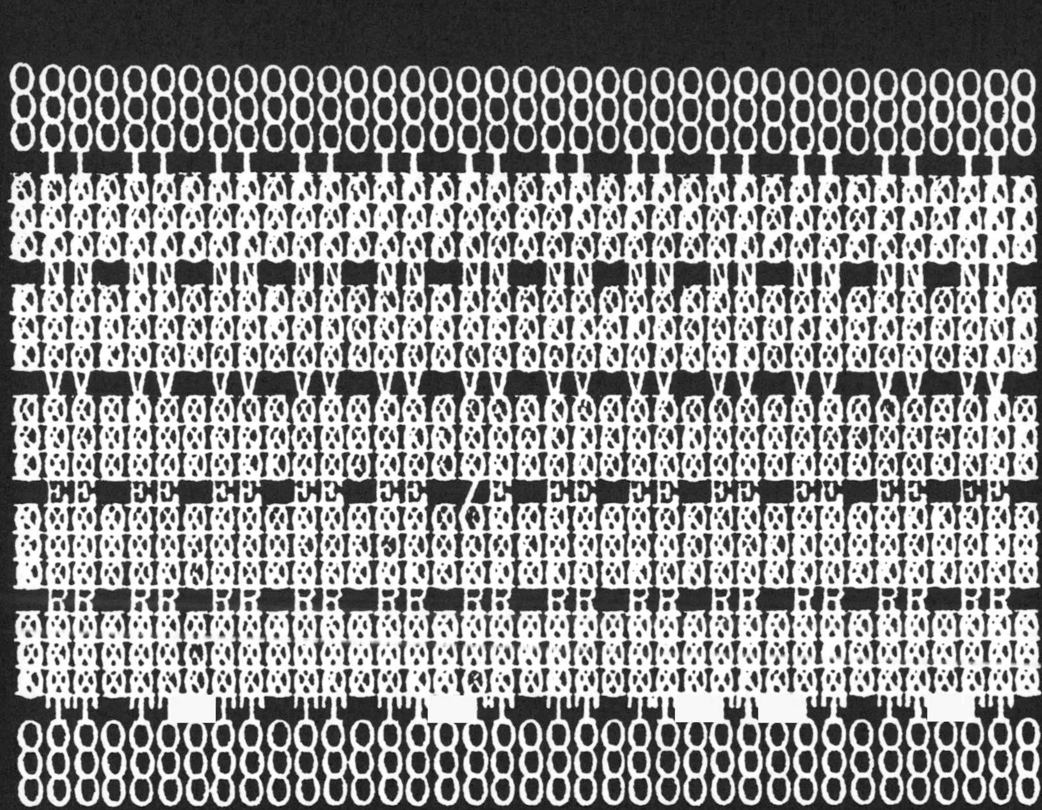

CHORUS :

rest a

measure

the bottom falls out
WHO / what is the bottom
WHO / what keeps it WHERE

CHORUS :

rest a

measure

spring & chaos in the air in yr workplace, at the festival, in the offices of yr friends, neighbors, loved ones, former housemates, in yr institutions, relations, desires, I take it in, in strides, as I'm updated, by the hours, by the books of ours, growing grasses haven't told me what they're growing they don't have to, the ceiling ripped open, unusual for buildings built of this era, somewhat stilted, or patchwork of nettings, or skins splayed as if newly applied, a kind of self-(re)generation or unintentional entrance, doorway or function, or flow of water, or seminal liquids, falling from a /

bove the bower or

a nightstand there i

s something moving

can can

hear it

pick the flowers over fumes / four-to-the-floor for Sunday noons / a pre-lunch drinks situation ground green grass golden in showers feeding off dandelion wild, even wilted, leaves full force, in yellows, made a wine, so hesitant, to reach out into an ether, a void, that is, avoidance, a boy, that is, a boy dance, losing a self heading straight into source of smell is neither bad nor enviable as position, fallen two steps behind, this waltz off key, notes too distant to settle, the stillness in the evening light still, some say, stiller, roots won't sit once plucked, tooth moving deep into a center, no gap in this dirt til we make it, the jasmine dried from the holy city, in the book itself a relic, these trees don't grow here anymore, haven't for a while, let it sit on the counter, on the right page, at the right time, itself begins to flower, a resonance of muscle, a memory of encounter, setting pace in tasteful measure, deepest as surrenders, the slow spit the spit still lowers, alone with you is how we'll grow it, tending to the end bits with a nibble, around the thing, a meditation on circumference, what light is that those flailing pinks draped against the woods of the crossing or the red stick poking out from the fronds, what harboring soundscape blistered in what mists aplenty the structure stabilized the line keeps growing it's alive in its own animate desires / in the dream of burgeoning vision / while napping on the greens the river & its guard will warn not to drink of its waters they've been growing fibers from plastics / in the new language of secrets call it a science of withholding scenery there is backslang & cant & the lingua franca dips in & out of common usage each ph(r)ase growing the plenty of a dialectic possibility / with each new stream new branch new stone a myriad of potential new acts arise from the backslant of the garden of the cruise of t /

his trade

this trick

this cove

ogle

/

/

splinter won't soften waiting for the blockage to pass means an awareness that this somehow might not last rising from the feet and the fingertips of the left side or through tendons upstream veins flowing can mind it as it winds in the pathways with no hint of sun trying modest days and softened flights harvests that may not hallow / brights the skin turned up an absence of wood boxes in the mold to be made are not yet boxes at all but mere blueprint eat something why don't you like recurring dreams or the stamina for such a garden or the wind that's found its way inside the room thought locked / finger how fraught my singular apologies I was sure I'd softened the nature of the thing its reaches immeasurable touching deep toward beaches uninhabitable gust of kin rust and din doesn't matter if you tilt the fling let it play a while fabric as / bolts cover this house as kind of shield to breathe the mark on the door or the friends in the walls or scurry on the rooftop through the nights *I won't push you / a promise / let you find your own way out* or in as dissolve collective

/

/

CHORUS : *[in trappings at the limit]*

(ALL

POWER

/

2 THE

PEOPLE)

CHORUS : *[extend the skin of it]*

/

/

thank you

/

hi o   I yawn o gape

stand open   pause

connect   badly

amazed   in wonder

bawl out   utter   sing

/

last   time was

fun my   cracks

are still   leaking

of anther   a kind of

lotion   let   breed

/

hi are   you open

for gape   pause

connect   badly

breath is   a kind of

excretion   utter   seed

/

thank you so dearly

/

this rabid
place dun-
smells geons
like & cell-
dried ars &
cum btt-
and ons of
sau- pryers
sage let gyre
burnt ass oc
limp iation

/

t hank you so dearly for all the night

/

touch

/

/

tuoch

/

/

tuch

/

/ /

tch

/ /

hank you so dearly for all the nigh
hank you so dearly for all the nigh
t hank you so dearly for all the nigh
hank you so dearly for all the nigh t
t hank you so dearly for all the nigh t
hank you so dearly for all the nigh t
t hank you so dearly for all the nigh t
hank you so dearly for all the nigh t
t hank you so dearly for all the nigh
hank you so dearly for all the nigh t
t hank you so dearly for all the nigh
hank you so dearly for all the nigh t
t hank you so dearly for all the nigh t
hank you so dearly for all the nigh t
t hank you so dearly for all the nigh
hank you so dearly for all the nigh t
t hank you so dearly for all the nigh t
hank you so dearly for all the nigh t
t hank you so dearly for all the nigh t
hank you so dearly for all the nigh t
t hank you so dearly for all the nigh t
hank you so dearly for all the nigh t
t hank you so dearly for all the nigh t
hank you so dearly for all the nigh t
t hank you so dearly for all the nigh t
hank you so dearly for all the nigh t
t hank you so dearly for all the nigh t
hank you so dearly for all the nigh t
t hank you so dearly for all the nigh t
hank you so dearly for all the nigh t
t hank you so dearly for all the nigh t
hank you so dearly for all the nigh t
t hank you so dearly for all the nigh t
hank you so dearly for all the nigh t
t hank you so dearly for all the nigh t
hank you so dearly for all the nigh t
t hank you so dearly for all the nigh t
hank you so dearly for all the nigh t
t hank you so dearly for all the nigh t
hank you so dearly for all the nigh t
t hank you so dearly for all the nigh t
hank you so dearly for all the nigh t
t hank you so dearly for all the nigh t
hank you so dearly for all the nigh t
t hank you so dearly for all the nigh t
hank you so dearly for all the nigh t
t hank you so dearly for all the nigh t
hank you so dearly for all the nigh t
t hank you so dearly for all the nigh t
hank you so dearly for all the nigh t
t hank you so dearly for all the nigh t
hank you so dearly for all the nigh t
t hank you so dearly for all the nigh t
hank you so dearly for all the nigh t
t hank you so dearly for all the nigh
hank you so dearly for all the nigh
hank you so dearly for all the nigh
hank you so dearly for all the nigh

/

around and around slip thru folds beneath rest a test under hirsute skies aplenty sip

/

a deep slink to stink a blessing phrase <softer than> once baby's [...] has grown tough

/

in this clime wear could tear flung open once as sore as puncture 4 one moment spread

/

in glory parted rivers seas an eagle let them dance like in Chicago fingers splaying

/

whole fists on the couch of a familiar apartment in Brooklyn were made private by the

/

bastion to the bedroom walls are not walls in this demolition of my submission ready

/

at the right time in the right place I am emptied of all prior consumption pull the arch

/

in the figure out this etching repoussé in dreams of internal hammering come full

/

flight wings spread at lengths unholy as an exorcism of my needs revealed as

/

apocalypse here on this scroll hear yr name as an indication of my ecstasies there is

/

the sex act there is that beyond the sex act there is little to no difference as in one and

/

the same as in when the rain comes in and the mountains roar and the ground so wet

/

it might slip beneath me holding on ever so tight under my feet with my soles barely

/

gripping there is the bare life and there is the manner in which a life is lived its quality

/

its textures its music like the passage from biopower to bottom power to power bottom

/

to bio bottom in this ecosystem without states but only pleasures crossing without

/

subjugations merely active submissions ready at the right time in the right place with

/

the right refusals of the spectacle of matter the acknowledgement of preservation as a

/

tactic might be read as a positive indeed the focus on life as opposed to the sovereign

/

threat of death indeed a new technology indeed a kind of analytics can we exist

/

outside power or past the fringes of acceptable speech refusing entrance to the caves

/

or meadows or beaches of the ligament where this finger meets this finger meets this

/

nail this sharp ending not an ending but the middle of the idle thing not playing but

/

being played praying to be betrayed or something else like trust or the kind of love

/

surrounding us as collective or as kinship or gay mafia an awareness of the thing each

/

relation albeit fraught so tender keep in check all that are with me in sickness and in

/

health in edgetimes and on the straight and narrow whole beds of communal presence

/

be you here or there or elsewhere nowhere I feel you still sloping by the virgule that

/

I'm using that I'm cruising by the pines or by the waters in the rusted irons that were

/

useful once were put in use once this little sloping haunt this bit of punctuation of the

/

line or for my breath to pause a moment lay still a moment without you feels so strange

/

as though this bay is not this bay without you not this gay without you weighing me

/

down, the outside feel my body sloping at the thought of it sloping wrought at the

/

moment of collective loss considerate sloping let me dwell on this dwelling swell on

/

the bare matter of factness of an ending holds no ending the paths that fill me

/

deeper dig deeper keep tending not just myself but these grasses my friends

/

exposed by the force of it the nope of this here graph the joke of this here

/

wrath the choke of it at the close steep in direction in ascension growing toward

/

this clime there's no end to this drive beg no head to it after that is after

/

he passed a dread to it tagged fake Pettibon to a wall there's no men / d to it

ch/eek

SH!T

CUM

SPIT

BLOOD

GUTS

/

metallic as shit
play on the
tongue

I know exactly
what's wrong
with the soup

and can't say it
but will here

anyway

the taste of
bile on the way
up

/

make it
simple call
me hole

/

verdant for
a minute or
the right rot

waiting for a
cyst to pop the
gall to flop

/

it burns

don't it

feel good

/

rest a

measure

ASSHOLE

SHALOES

ASHSLOE

head to the bed of
the (breathe) bed
head to the head of
the (breathe) bed
of the (breathe) bed
to the head to the
(breathe) head to
the (breathe) bed
to the bed of the
(breathe) head to
the (breathe) bed
to the (breathe)
head to the
(breathe) head to
the (breathe) head
to the (breathe)
bed to the (breathe)
bed to the (breathe)
head to the bed to
the (breathe) head
to the (breathe) to
the (breathe) head
to the bed to the
(breathe) to the
(breathe) to the
(breathe) to the
bed to the (breathe)
head to the bed of
the (breathe) bed
head to the head of
the (breathe) bed
of the (breathe) bed
to the head to the
(breathe) head to
the (breathe) bed
to the bed of the
(breathe) head to
the (breathe) bed
to the (breathe)
head to the
(breathe) head to
the (breathe) head
to the (breathe)
bed to the (breathe)
bed to the (breathe)
head to the bed to
the (breathe) head

SOHEALS

OLASHES

Ɇ ø SLASH

SOLEASH

HASSOLE

AHSLOES

HOLESAS

LASSOHE

LOSESHA

H O

É SO S

HÉLAS

L S

A

head to the bed of
to the head to the
the (breathe) bed
(breathe) head to
head to the head of
the (breathe) bed
the (breathe) bed
to the bed of the
of the (breathe) bed

bed to the (breathe)
(breathe) head to
head to the bed to
the (breathe) head
the (breathe) head
to the (breathe)
to the (breathe) to
bed to the (breathe)
the (breathe) head
bed to the (breathe)
to the bed to the
head to the bed to
(breathe) to the
the (breathe) head
(breathe) to the
to the (breathe) to
(breathe) to the
the (breathe) head
bed to the (breathe)
head to the bed of
(breathe) to the
the (breathe) bed
(breathe) to the
head to the head of
(breathe) to the
the (breathe) bed
bed to the (breathe)
of the (breathe) bed
head to the bed of
to the head to the
the (breathe) bed
(breathe) head to
head to the head of
the (breathe) bed
the (breathe) bed
to the bed of the
of the (breathe) bed
(breathe) head to
to the head to the
the (breathe) bed
(breathe) head to
to the (breathe)
the (breathe) bed
head to the
to the bed of the
(breathe) head to
(breathe) head to
the (breathe) head
the (breathe) bed
to the (breathe)
to the (breathe)
bed to the (breathe)
head to the
bed to the (breathe)
(breathe) head to
head to the bed to
the (breathe) head
the (breathe) head
to the (breathe)
to the (breathe) to
bed to the (breathe)
the (breathe) head
bed to the (breathe)
to the bed to the
head to the bed to
(breathe) to the
the (breathe) head
(breathe) to the
to the (breathe) to

rest a

measure

/

Gemini

in orgasm

chop an inch

off the page

feed slow

steady, gentle

a suite in

a cave, mark

a presence

wake, there

is no there,

there, the two

sucking off

each ear

/

Uranian

contr action

self shatter

dripping

/

„wrest”

from the text

„read a”

loud

/

TEND AIR

HOLE DAWN

OLIVE A
BOUGHT UM

/

„quicker”

now from a

„deep sea”

ted breath

/

PEN A TRAY

SHUN GNAT

THULL EVOL UV

THULL ET ER

/

/

„asking"

now for

„active part"

icipation

/

UH SOD UH

ME UV SILL

UH BULLS UP RICK

UH SENSE AY SHUN

/

„can I"

hear or

„deep in"

side or

/

EYE ONE

TUBE EEEEE

ILL LEDGE

A BULL

/

„in the"

Song that

„Spenser"

likes

/

/ /

hear

DANS TON PANTALON, BITES D'ANIMAUX

/

ROTO PANTALÓN, ¡GRITANDO!

for

/ /

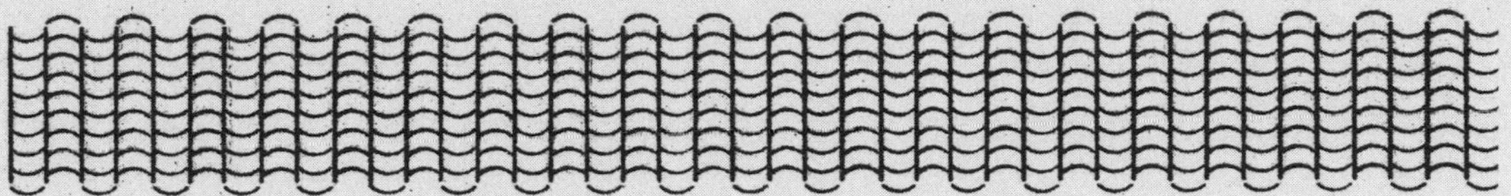

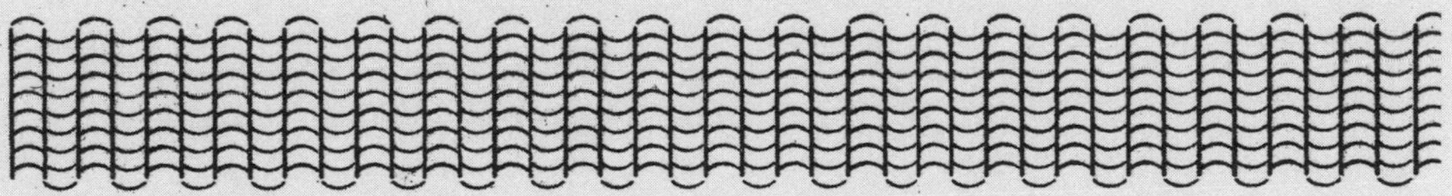

/

brittle shivers I can't hide from riddled fritters up the sides or / the animal supply box full of false dyes mixed the hues to turn nothing at all / heavy like a wet sweater the glove too big to slip on one coat over soft heather the child of a minor fealty / digestion is the bottoming of the gut & its inverse in relation to position in the path of organic matter / through a system whose pathways stretch to absorb encompass welcome nourishment in the form of proteins / this is more than mere empathic vibes rather hark a call to care work / end each text with x's and o's here a kiss there a hug cross the networks that someday will fill us / thinking there should be a language centered practice around eating I put red paprika on my rice pasta / to live with restrictions is to play with more of the same, open to the mere possibility of the possible, anything near me edible / I read this Facebook post where a certain Doug I don't know posits that we can end capitalism, corporate hold over land, water particularly those unceded looking at you Nestlé & even save the earth by spraying vegetables with nicotine / getting people addicted to salad & this Doug really got me when noting what this would do to our collective gut health / got me thinking what roughage does to my system, really fucks me, for a good minute, a day, maybe more, but what if / I just need more of it, an addiction, or a craving, a desire, a heap of it / in me at all times, keep coming, in me / the day so full I can't take lunch I'm eating these books I'm pricing / eating the stock I'm moving / drowning under piles of a kind of printed matter / fills me in editions critical in a language of the moment now & never past & present / if you zoom out it's beautiful can see the whole process sw

/

immingly / like from where the highways merge under the particular / megalotto signage where it smells always / of sulphur it's / a shower with E in Iceland / or a geothermic hotspot / again I'm naked / taking / it in / again / a raw / power / the label of his beer says something apocalyptic one of those "just a speck" kind of lines has the title of the Hopkins poem about Digby it's the "beginning of the end" of times I guess but not my favorite : "even your unpassion'd eyelids might be wet" / the aesthetc takes in taste / bottoms beauty / everything out of the woodquirks / the book is / asshole I cruise thru I am / the book / everyone / out of their woodquirks a / hole to see the sky thru is / still a hole to see / the sky thru says Rot(h) or Yoko Ono / Rot(h) to Yoko Ono / one an asshole owned / the other for the sky / restricted / access / there are no restrictions when / the hole is made many / folds to this book / the hole is the book / the spread of the pages / lay open / spread the pages / crease the fold / to the eye o / pen at the fold / in the privacy of a home / or on the subway / in the park / at the old cruising spot / the excitement at feeling o / pen feeling sp / read / I buy a typewriter on the internet, an Olivetti Dora, I want to feel each key press the page, tender, sometimes harder, sometimes drill it, when it comes the carriage won't unlock, I can jump across one line vertical, from top to bottom override it, a store nearby takes the bottom off immediately, finds my issue, it's the space bar, engaged & mid-working, cuts the problem open, from the bottom, from the bottom I can make these little books to distribute, it's a project of immediacy, from my bedroom, sitting in the backyard, it takes one sheet and one sheet only, the project is one of produci

/

/

ng, an object unique in practice, as in, each sheet must be typed alone, with its own characters, an alignment original, the game is one of space, of orientation, each page distinct, a one night stand, some of the same moves, inverted, transposed, a novel relation, I use symbols, slashes, zeroes, the same letter, manually, the carriage drops a little lower, drops a little, 1/1 is how I call them, one of one, I could say one over one, one over the other, it's all the same, in the name of the project, I bind them, thread & a sewing needle, prick them, let them prick me, I draw blood, in the name of the project, it's all the same, I wear them til they become with me, of me, as in, the emergence of a ritual, two or three a day, I pass them out, myself I pass out, in the streets, behind the counter, at the bookstore, for Lindsay, Colter, Jeff, Kalie, Trisha, Jane, Owen, let myself open, at the folds, at my back, a signature, date, myself, the earthquake rattles out a forgotten premonition, messy, make myself, a bad reader, lost in hairs, a suite of stragglers, open to the line to its permutations to the possibility inherent in an arrangement, a correspondence, the machine behind the shapes, it is pounding, the page, as well as, myself, pounding, these days I'm only playing with toys that have keys, making a mess of them, pounding, incessantly, pounding, snap my ribbon, pounding, resound, a recognition of the letter, making sewns I puncture a series of O's with a needle and thread, I contradict the terms of the page, of writing, of myself, this is an engagement not contractual, but felt, make it tangible, a process, feel it out, I bottom, fucked, over, and over, again, fuck, over, and over, again, extending what is felt, to an audience, in this case of one, in this case,

/ O

of many, sewing us, together, binding us, together, through the word, across the page, by the letter, I am littered, in threads, connecting, my bed, to my sweater, to the vowel, to the capital, letter, together, sewing us, binding us, letter by letter, geometric, in forms, shaped, by desire, inescapable, this string, this bit, from my mouth, hanging, out like a leash, to the head, of the bed, cross the blades, of a back, to the thighs, of this book, to its ankles, bound, together, in a line, from the neck, down the spine, hear the thread snap, together, hear the thread snap, with pleasure, a tickle in a throat, in the guts, a spread, the space of a page, a landscape erotic, of desire, these letters, I fill, I puncture, active, needle, needle, active, thread, string, knot, a tripartite action, for the book, in three parts, the bottom, cheek, hole, cheek, I make many holes, space emphatically, plural, in process, plural, in dynamic, the colors I've confused, in language, cross strings, cross streams, along the lines of capital, letters, littered, in primary, secondary, colors, this hole, marked, for knotting, this hole, marked, to share, hands, on every part, of production, distribution, the (w)hole assembly, line threading knots, through a larger, web, of entanglements, since found myself swimming, in spiders, that won't drown nor, I, nor these holes, nor these books, that won't drown, nor, I, in the space, of capital, letters, direct my, attention, my, possible, entrapments, direct, desire, or the path, or its potentials, sewing, a bottom, open, flowing, across a landscape, erotic, of desire, inescapable, it has been written, knotted, tied, the edges cut, the fluff fluffed, readied, for a night out, a pocket squeeze, with capital, letters, screaming for capital, littered, tied, how tight, can bear

/

///

binding exercises :

/// ///

ROUS [ROUS ROUS ROUS ROUS ROUS ROUS ROUS]

/// ///

spell 84 : for a man to obtain a male lover [p. 177-78]

text : ashmolean museum 1981 : 940

description : vellum, 8x10.5 cm, originally folded to 2.5 x 1.3 cm (by the evidence of creases) ; perhaps 6th century

/// ///

+CELTATALBABAL [.]KARASHNEIFE[.]NNAS'KNEKIE

, BY THE POWER OF YAO SABAOTH,

ROUS ROUS ROUS ROUS ROUS ROUS ROUS ROUS

/// ///

or : anonymous verse (Com. Adesp. fr. 12) / class antagonisms :

'everyone long-haired is pollinated'

[be as bee to me – who were wealth / leisured young men – katapugon & the dactyl – the finger in phallic resonance invokes its obverse – the rump or buttocks of classical studies – one stressed, two unstressed paint a picture – of comedy the sausage seller & the katapugon's passing fart – an omen of anatomy altered – parsed through the very sound of it – in passing all present attached to it – in passing all present bound – the anatomy roused to subsume – the anatomy roused to attach – from the navel through the entrails bound – to the seller, be the smell that binds us – be long-haired as /// smell as bee to me /////////]

(Aristophanes, *The Knights*)

CHORUS :

rest a

measure

unrestrained in

all desires

measure

rest a

CHORUS :

VERS
ATIL
EVER
SATI
LEVE
RSAT
ILEV
/ ERSA
TILE
VERS
O O O O O O O O O O O O O O O O ATIL O O O O O O O O O O O O O O O O O
O O O O O O O O O O O O O O O O EVER O O O O O O O O O O O O O O O O O
O O O O O O O O O O O O O O O O SATI O O O O O O O O O O O O O O O O O
LEVE
RSAT
ILEV /
ERSA
TILE
VERS
ATIL
EVER
SATI
LEVE
RSAT
ILEV
ERSA
TILE

/

find the form a spread / of cheeks across mutant / materials a mess of plastics / neon or assemblage / in places threads of paper, metals, hairs, etc. / there's a pose to this card lay of

flesh / at the bot / tom of

the basket / breaking boys behind / all this

to say / the muse is a dom top / the poet / hole / greedy

/

/ /

some
thing
like
the
(p)lay
of
teeth
across
regions

earth
cave
lick
tip
sweet
turn
tart
air
metal

/ /

/

for threads to this meeting / a head to this greeting / capital forms the vertices to gape

in the making a play / of writing that is not writing / rather make it take shape in this

house not a house but a host / for a needle in a haystack / can can see it can can feel it

/

/ SOFTE BUTT
NSOFT ERBU
ENSOF O TTER
TENSO BUTT
FTENS O O ERBU
OFTEN TTER
SOFTE O O BUTT
NSOFT ERBU
ENSOF O O TTER
TENSO BUTT
FTENS O O ERBU
OFTEN TTER
SOFTE O O BUTT
NSOFT ERBU
ENSOF O O TTER
TENSO O O BUTT
FTENS ERBU
O OFTEN TTER O
SOFTE BUTT
O NSOFT ERBU O
ENSOF TTER
O TENSO BUTT O
FTENS ERBU
O OFTEN TTER O
SOFTE BUTT
O NSOFT ERBU O
ENSOF TTER
O O O O O TENSO O O O O O O O O O O O BUTT O O O O O
FTENS ERBU
OFTEN TTER /

/

pricking at the tip of this sp / read at the edges of a p / age at the dissolution of my fantasies / str / etching me slowly / gentle at the gr / asp there is the word it is calling from a higher place / from a lower place / from the ceiling from the bow

/

/

]
gag
am
gag
ged
[

/

/

els of a blessing can can h / ear it / can can sense it at the tip / of a tongue or the rim
of a ba / sin receptive / to the son / ics of a sen / tence as it changes as it / glazes over
mean / ings and the bind / ings they've ex / tend / ed themselves from the spin

/

SEE PAS
KSE SPA
EKS SSP
EEK ASS
SEE PAS
KSE SPA
EKS SSP
/ EEK ASS
SEE PAS
KSE SPA
EKS SSP
OO OO OO OO OO OO OO
EEK ASS
SEE PAS
KSE SPA
EKS SSP
OO OO OO OO OO OO
EEK ASS
SEE PAS
KSE SPA
EKS SSP
OO OO OO OO OO OO OO
EEK ASS
SEE PAS
KSE SPA
EKS SSP
EEK ASS /
SEE PAS
KSE SPA
EKS SSP
EEK ASS
SEE PAS
KSE SPA
EKS SSP
/ EEK ASS

e to the sp / ace of the p / age they've ass / erted themselves in the mid

dle of a mind or a land / scape ero / tic plucking me plucking

my th / read / s to the edge of this c / limb / to the edge of the

/

/ /

drive
into
fjords
as
ground
in
heat
deep
feed
as
extra

down
like
low
to
water
raw
these
greens
lean
in
labor

/ /

/

c / limb / t / his her / e cliff a pro / spect / a cle / a / ring /

D / EAT / H / DE / AT / H / DE / ATH / DEA / TH / D / EATH /

c / licking of / f a pin's / fee

/

/

SPIN
ESPI
NESP
O INES O
PINE
SPIN
ESPI
O NESP O
INES
PINE
SPIN
O ESPI O
NESP
INES
PINE O O
O SPIN O O
ESPI O O
NESP
INES
O PINE O
SPIN
ESPI
O NESP O
INES
PINE
SPIN
O ESPI O
NESP
INES
PINE

/

/

ding off Wor(l)ds / taking them in the p / lot

thickens / hairy / the further in t / his fore / st the

deeper the t / horns / cut / the need / les prick a h / and

/

/ /

vitriol alchemical
green as vast
desires
compress exhumation
complex preservation
f(l)ailing
one [ ] of one
weight to melt for

eighth in flask
to form seal for
err(or)s
being celestial
know names

attributes ofservice
one [ ] of one
of
over the other
feel me under
stigma(ta)
the weight of
a name [.]

/
/

/

a finger / a tip / the can / opy re / strict / s the vi / ew in

the hol / low t / urns / il / leg / ible / the let / ters / twist the

body s / pins / rig / ht round / t / urn me / right roun / d

/

CHORUS :

rest a

measure

WAKE UP to friendship

intimate LOVING friendship

NOTHING gayer

CHORUS :

rest a

measure

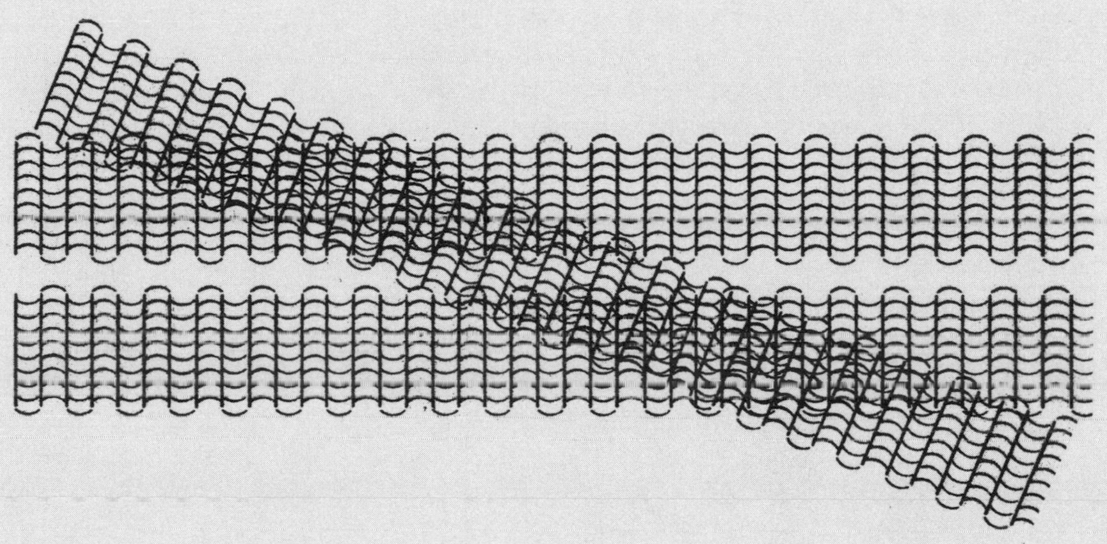

/

On the call with T who's thinking through holes, we want to take them out of lack, when the unknown is full, of a kind of potential, the depths carry with them new landscapes of affective, of potential relation, if the abstract is neither abstract nor concrete, but rather only validated, made manifest, through a series of social relations, what factors mark a hole less real than say, the cock, less full of swelling, potential outbursts, of say, the physicality of production, to bottom not to be filled but to envelop to embrace to engage, the distinction between a hard & soft g, not a *giraffe* but a guillotine, *gay*, notable : *gangrene*, which might explain my confusion regarding the pronunciation of that kind of file I've been using, that is the *gif* or *jif* as I sometimes hear it, while the soft /dʒ/ was the intention of the format's inventor, the hard /g/ is widespread, and also valid, there's a rule about certain vowels following the letter that dictate the sound, I had this conversation recently, someone hadn't heard of the great vowel shift, I wonder if there could be another, how long it could take when I wanted it yesterday, T's been permanently banned from the country, that last deportation, explained as administrative error, now seems like a cover-up, or even a ploy, to get T across certain borders, it's so fucked up, I say over the computer, over the social media overlord's netspace, where the same agents who had spent months pouring over T's data, forcibly given, are still listening, would a vowel shift help, or is there more need for a new kind of language, bring back Polari, P might learn Lubunca, we joke about bottoming for the state but it isn't funny, the degree to which an undesired, nonconsensual exposure, seizure, of the extens

/

ions of a body, its inner workings, its network of relations, getting an endoscopy was both natural & unnatural, I desired the camera, wanted it to enter my pathways, blow up my colon on the big screen, know what I (don't) know, it didn't matter whether the instrument went down my throat or up from my bottom, it was all the same, there's a storied trope of str8 asshole disgust with a fair dose of fear there, everyone asking me whether I'd be ok, if I was comfortable with what the procedure, could entail, like that viral moment, where people started writing, about the str8 men in their lives refusing to touch their own holes, to the extent that after shitting, they'd rather leave skid marks, across all fabrics, than touch themselves, than clean themselves, I'd find it sad if I didn't find it so funny, even pathetic, I can feel mine by the hour, it is speaking, I have this feeling, to get back to this sense of lack, that so pervades my fair organ, a kind of drive, to points of pain, of cuties, leaving bits of pieces, around me, to make relic, this one, in particular, as vial, so perfect, empty, with a top of cork, I could play it, it was never waiting, to be filled, but already, full of meaning, that is, to say, that anything, placed inside it, over-determined, a new kind of meaning, when my joy was in its potential manifestations, out of thin air, as if, out of thin air, as if, there are many routes from one pleasure, one point of pleasure, many routes together, that can flow together, in the space of this hole, in this ground, at the base, of where it starts, in the belly of the beast, like how one could give away all their books in the act of flirting, by the handful, by the load, letting them lay, heavy, I relinquish myself, to a feeling, interrupted, reverberating, from the roof of a mo

/

/

uth to the pillow, it makes me (w)hole, symmetric, spanning positions, both/and, spanning, universals & particulars, instead of something, with another bringing, out a kind of kinetic frenzy, frenetic kind of crazy, I forget how to write or, maybe, taken over, this language not my intention, the feeling even less so, mine, there is no agency, to the matter, an intensity, of vibration, from the bowel, to the bottom of the page, the act of shitting it, of language, taken in me, from external source, the act of shitting it, of contradictory use, that is, directionally speaking, ambiguous, or like, something, off, this one key, a few octaves above me, oscillating, today flat, tomorrow just a bit, sharp, subtle, I can feel it in my, bones, through my skin, between my ears, spanked, at the rear, of the car, or the hydraulic mess, wet with it, the dissonance, out of body, out of mind, out of tune, the dissonance, that is, the science, of flow, the erotic, etymologically, more accurate, alternatively, in compounds, to pour forth, to vomit, waking up with headache and chills, the knot in my neck travels, with each morning, downward, through my shoulders, blades, upper back, settles, somewhere in the middle, past my most ambitious reaches, lightheaded, again, not out of lack, but from the crushing power of it, all, taking it all, in, overwhelming, in strides I recognize, I need, the Frank poem "Digression On Number 1, 1948" : *"I am ill today but I am not / too ill. I am not ill at all. / It is a perfect day, warm / for winter, cold for fall."* to touch his perfect hand, not Pollock's, there wasn't enough gossip amongst poets this season, so I made myself object, willingly, its subject, the lines again, blurred, the staves, of letters, or the space for music, or, woo

/

d for the bed, making, an architecture of expressions, of gestures, bouncing along the line, across the page, on top of cities, hardwood, bodies, across four languages, Emmett Williams globes with inner globes, his Guardian Angel, evades, try to find it for a select number of loved ones, it hides in stacks, among other angels, a small chapbook from '85, the spheres bounce and grow across sixteen pages, including covers, carrying the subtitle : *aktiv–passiv* ; *actif–passif* ; *active–passive* ; *attivo–passivo* ; a want to read a secret hidden, in an en dash, slightly wider than a hyphen, narrower than an em dash, as in, here, a span or range, typical of numbers, to read to or through, active through passive, to passive, a progression, complication to, the farce of a binary, myth of a dualism, balls and holes growing, along the line, across the page, protector, of position, or together, an icon, a vision, to state, some stakes, in a matter, am the mere letter, hidden, yet legible, encircled, in sphere, boundless, in motion, across the page, across the reader's, gaze, swirling, in vain, forget how to write, never knew, am lettered, keyed, anal, retentive, wet with it, did remember to lock, the front door, the gate, the shop, when we close, am never, closed, wet with it, lettered, keyed, anal, attentive, staying open, perpetually, open, naked, in the hope of speaking, directly, that is, orbit, a rotation, an axis, solar, in, anus, in, the heat of it, letting slip, self, name, what's in, self, in, ass, oh that, lettered, keyed, interpreted, the vision, many years ago, of the most, self, dried, shriveled, read as nut, see now, pure, hole, the skin cracked, dented, round the edges, as it folds, into self, pure, hole, lettered, keyed, misinterpreted, true, self, true, hole, breathe, in, give, the final,

/

A

that

H

off

H

H

hole

kilter

H

H

that

be

H

H

is

nt

H

acknowledgments

An enormity of grace & love to those who brought this book to life with me, through living it, speaking it, caressing it & me, my mentors, friends, collaborators, and loved ones : Trisha Low, Owen Hill, Lindsay Choi, Evan Kennedy, Eric Sneathen, Jane Gregory, Pırıltı Onukar, Kalie McGuirl, Jerry Thompson, Alec Şaşati, Violet Spurlock, Terry Taplin, Angus Reid, Eli Petzold, Thomas Keys, Dion Kauffman.

This book would not have been possible without the generous attention of the staff at Nightboat. Thank you Stephen Motika, Lindsey Boldt, Caelan Ernest, Kazim Ali, and Andrea Abi-Karam for believing in this work and gifting it with materiality. And many thanks to Rissa Hochberger for typesetting this monster of a book.

Deepest respect for the editors who've released excerpts thus far : Barrett White, H. V. Cramond, Dylan Byron. And gratitude to *MARY: A Journal of New Writing* for publishing "the pressure of holding sphincter" and the Academy of American Poets for publishing "echium swallows" in their Poem-a-Day series. My thanks to Brian Blanchfield for selecting that piece for publication.

& to the late Kevin Killian, whose interest in this work sparked flirtation, gossip, and the dream of a photograph, a ghost image. It's all for you.

+ as always, Spenser.

NOAH ROSS is a bookseller, editor, and poet based in Berkeley, CA. The author of *Swell*, Noah edits *Baest: a journal of queer forms & affects* and, with Lindsay Choi, Mooon/IO.

NIGHTBOAT BOOKS

Nightboat Books, a nonprofit organization, seeks to develop audiences for writers whose work resists convention and transcends boundaries. We publish books rich with poignancy, intelligence, and risk. Please visit nightboat.org to learn about our titles and how you can support our future publications.

The following individuals have supported the publication of this book. We thank them for their generosity and commitment to the mission of Nightboat Books:

Kazim Ali
Anonymous (4)
Jean C. Ballantyne
The Robert C. Brooks Revocable Trust
Amanda Greenberger
Rachel Lithgow
Anne Marie Macari
Elizabeth Madans
Elizabeth Motika
Thomas Shardlow
Benjamin Taylor
Jerrie Whitfield & Richard Motika

In addition, this book has been made possible, in part, by grants from the National Endowment for the Arts, the New York City Department of Cultural Affairs in partnership with the City Council, the New York State Council on the Arts Literature Program, and the Topanga Fund.

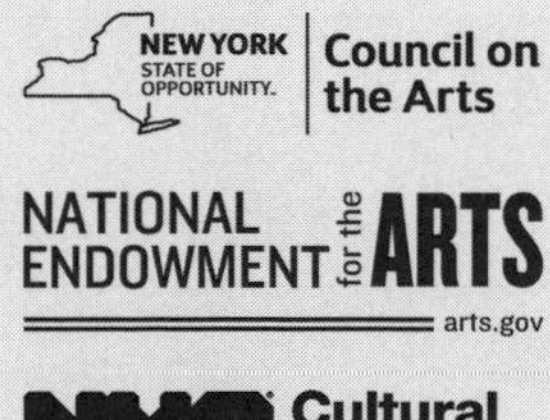

NYC Cultural Affairs